RELIGION THROUGH REASON

Books by Ernest L. Ramer

Religion Through Reason
The Catholic Church of the Future

Religion
Through Reason

by ERNEST L. RAMER

EXPOSITION PRESS   HICKSVILLE, NEW YORK

Contents

Introduction

At this time many things are happening to the human race. The feeling of security that has existed here in the United States of America for almost two hundred years is being severely tested. At all levels even the loyalty of some of our political leaders is not what should be expected from the leaders of our government. The people of the United States have put their faith and trust in those people they voted into high offices in our government. Large corporations, which we have depended on for many years to help make the United States a good country to live in, have given in to the fallacy of excessive profits without any regard for the people who depend on them for food and other manufactured products.

Along with this feeling of insecurity, through the actions of government leaders and business leaders, many people begin to question other ideas and principles that we have followed for many years, even many centuries. There seems to be a feeling among individuals that how a person wants to live is a matter of choice for each one of us. Whatever a person wants to do seems to be the decision that makes anything all right. Even in their religious beliefs, many people think that any way they desire to believe about our creator, God, is permissible.

Because of our free will, this idea is permitted by God Himself. It is only through self-respect that a person realizes that he had better do the best he can for himself as he goes through life. No other human being can do it for him. Each one of us must depend on ourselves individually to live our lives the best way we can. When we cannot solve the many problems that we must face while living on earth, and when no other human being can help us, what other way is there to get help?

Through reason we can understand that God, our supernatural creator, is the last resort for us to go to for help. This book is for those people who would like to take a look at God from the point of view of reason, considering the world as we find it today.

Juvenile delinquents are one of the most important groups of individuals who need to make good decisions as to how they shall continue to live their lives. Already they find themselves misguided by the adults they have imitated. Now is the time for them to remember that every one of them belongs to God Himself. In spite of what any person or book tells them, teenagers are created by God and are therefore responsible to God, not to people. Christ in the Blessed Sacrament is there to help every juvenile delinquent who goes to the Church where the Blessed Sacrament is found. It is only by making visits to Christ in the Blessed Sacrament in the Church that all people can gradually understand that, in some way or other, an unseen supernatural power is there to help them. That profound peace of mind that can be found where Christ is present in the Blessed Sacrament, is possible only through supernatural power.

The course of the Catholic Church in the future will continue, with the Mass the same as it was when Christ performed it at the Last Supper. The reason that the Catholic Church will continue as long as the Earth survives is that the supernatural presence of Christ exists in the Blessed Sacrament or Holy Eucharist. Christ is the reason for the Catholic Church. It is perfectly evident in the history of Christ on earth that Christ said, "This is my body and my blood. Unless you eat of my body and drink of my blood, you shall not have eternal life."

The proof of His supernatural presence is up to Christ Himself. Every person must seek the help of Christ for himself. No human being can bestow upon another person the supernatural help of Christ. It is just the same as when Christ was on earth. By His miracles, Christ helped those people who had complete faith in him.

Part One:

An Approach to Faith

RELIGION THROUGH REASON

There are many different religious organizations spread out over the entire world. Each one is different in the ideas and practices it believes and teaches. However, there are many things about which most of them agree. Those groups that base their beliefs on Christianity have many similar ideas about Christ and His life on earth. Other groups have different ideas about Christ and God.

This book about religion is not an attempt to study, analyze, or compare one religion with another. Since there is so much discussion about religion, even among the leaders of the numerous churches, it is easily understood that there is much confusion about religion. This just makes it all the more difficult for average people to know what to believe or how to practice their religion. If God wants us to serve Him and live the best way we can to please Him, then there should be some way for people to find ways and means of doing these things. God in His love and justice to His earthly creatures should have provided these things for mankind as they were needed for the human race. So our problem will be to attempt to reason out for ourselves some of the important things that God has done to help His creatures find out what He really expects them to do to serve Him. Also we should find out how to get the help from God or Christ that is so necessary for each one of us. We should find it possible to reason these important facts out in our minds.

It may be difficult to discuss some of the points we want to cover in what might be the best order. The main thing is to get the most important facts included in these pages.

To begin with, it is not hard for us to believe in a supernatural Creator. We are already here on earth. Human beings do not have the power to create anything, other than their own kind, and put life into it. So we can reason it out that some unseen and unknown Being has the tremendous power to make the world and all the creatures here. Thus we find ourselves under the influence and power of an unknown God. The way

11

God created the earth and the rest of the universe is a great
mystery to human beings, although through the study of the
earth, we are finding out some of the things that have occurred
in its history.

The manner in which God created human beings is something that God has a right to keep for His own knowledge. In
order to serve God we don't have to know how He created our
first parents. We can reason that God planned how He would
create human beings and then He made them just exactly as
He wanted them. We can believe that God does not make mistakes. He knows what the results will be before He creates anything. So He does not have to change anything He creates.

It is easy to understand that human beings are marvelous
creations of God. In spite of the hundreds of millions of people
on earth, no two persons are alike. No two lives are the same,
because their life experiences are never the same. However,
while each one of us is a distinct individual, the most important
reason for our existence on earth can be the same for everyone.
Living on earth was not meant by God to be an end in itself.
If this were true, then God in His justice would give every
person an equal chance in life by giving everyone the same op-
portunities and the same abilities. We can see that this is not
the way people are in this world. The earth merely affords the
place, the time, and the opportunity for human beings to serve
God the best way they can during their lives. The faithful servants of God will receive their reward from Him after death.
During their lives on earth, people have many problems to face.
It seems easy to believe the most important problem is their responsibility to themselves in trying to serve God to the best of
their ability.

Since we live in a world surrounded by earthly things, it is
hard for people to understand much about God and supernatural life. They are busy making a living for themselves or
helping people one way or another. That makes it all the easier,
more or less, to forget about God.

When a person does forget about God and seeks earthly
things and pleasures, he finds no lasting satisfaction in this way

of life. First he seeks one thing only to find that he still is not satisfied after he gets what looked so good before. Then he tries something else and that is the same. About the only satisfaction a person can have is that every other person is living under the same conditions. Is it possible that God created human beings in such a way that, regardless of how they live—if they live for the things and pleasures of this life—they can never find true peace and contentment on this earth? Why do people have such a strong urge to try to make the world a better place to live in? Why do they want their children to have an easier life than they have had? These things merely prove that the minds of people are focused on the ideas concerned with better living here, rather than on preparing for a life after death. It is reasonable to believe that regardless of how people live, as long as they live for the things of the earth, they will never be satisfied. Since God created mankind and the world just as He wanted them, we know He had a definite and real purpose in making everything just as it is. If people cannot find true peace and contentment with earthly things, what can they do? The only other course they can follow would be to try to follow God the best way they know how. Since God has the power to create human beings, He certainly has any kind of control over them that He might desire. As weak human beings we can't successfully fight God in any way. All we can do is make ourselves miserable trying. A creature of God is about as helpless as a grain of sand in fighting God. With our free will, we can either accept or fight against the course our life on earth follows under the direction of God. Many of our limitations are the direct result of the laws of nature established by our Creator Himself. Therefore, by following the laws of nature and submitting to the will of God we can enjoy peace of soul and mind. We will be much happier than if we try to live for earthly things.

Most of us have had enough experience in living to know that many times during our lives we have trials and troubles. What do we think about when there is no one to help us? Only the best of friends can give us even a little consolation. No earthly power seems to be of value to us. There seems to be nothing else to do but seek the help of God. Is God really interested in His weak and helpless creatures? These and many other questions come to our minds. Perhaps through reasoning we can find information for those people who are interested in learning more about God and His relationship with human beings.

God in His justice and love has made it possible for His creatures to find out how they can go to Him for the help that is so necessary for them. God gave us our free will but we must use it ourselves. So we turn to God for help through our own decision.

If just one person can find Jesus in the Blessed Sacrament through reading the information presented here, the effort will be well rewarded. Just remember you are free to choose just how far you will read in these pages and how you will accept it. God will allow you to make your own decision through your own free will.

Since our relationship with God is of great importance to us, we should be able to reason out the facts that will help us to understand what our real duties toward God are. Two of the greatest means of help God gave us are our conscience and our reasoning power. In seeking knowledge to serve God, a person is really helping himself. God doesn't need our help, but we certainly need His help. One way to present these things we need to understand is through reason by questions and answers. So we will use that way.

WILL GOD BE JUST IN HIS DEMANDS ON HUMAN BEINGS?

With a little faith in God, I believe we can begin with the feeling that He will be just in His demands on human beings. So if God requires us to believe anything that is important, He will let us know some way or other exactly what He expects us to do. One very important way that God controls and directs people is through nature and the laws of nature. God established the laws of nature and man cannot evade them. Also people cannot change natural laws. If the laws of nature are disregarded, man has to suffer the results that follow. God's justice toward His creatures is shown by the results that follow when people obey the natural laws rather than try to change or avoid them. For example, when a person is tired, nature tells him to rest. If he keeps on working without rest, his health will be affected. Then he will lose a whole lot more than he gained by working when he should have rested. This is an example of how his free will gets him in trouble—and God did not interfere.

It might seem at first that nature rebels right away against man's improper ways of living. That is not the case, because nature first tries to help man in spite of his wrong ways. It is only after prolonged efforts by human beings to disregard nature's laws that their bodies suffer permanent damage. Even nature is continually trying to help weak human beings. If we are trying to find out what God would have us do to serve Him, it will be easier for us to understand. For example: we know that God, as our Creator, has infinite power to help us. Therefore, we should turn to Him for help instead of depending on other human beings. Our intelligence tells us we are completely dependent on God for everything we may have to use on earth while we live here. If we can understand, or if we can learn from experience, then God has given us the means to try to turn to Him for help and consolation.

There are certain things that Christ told His followers while He was on earth and that we can believe without any doubt. History records the most important of these words of Christ that God wanted Him to tell human beings. These words of Christ were spoken so simply that anyone could understand what He meant.

The more people learn about how the earth is made and how

nature operates, the more they learn how completely dependent they are on God. This helps to prove the justice of God in His dealings with His creatures.

After creating man just as He wanted to, God gave him a free will. Thus each individual, through his free will can decide whether he wants to turn to God for help and guidance or not. If he forgets about God, his only choice is to depend on himself or some other person.

In His justice, God will never refuse to help anyone who asks Him for it. We can expect Him to do whatever is best for His creatures, not just what they ask Him for.

IS IT NECESSARY TO HAVE AN OPEN MIND IN OUR APPROACH TO RELIGION?

Supposing we have already decided that certain things we will believe and other things we won't believe. We may be right in all of them, or we may be mistaken in some of our ideas on religion. How did we arrive at the answers to questions of belief that we have already accepted? Maybe we arrived at our decisions after carefully thinking the proposition over. Or maybe we believed because some other person told us that we should believe certain things. Perhaps we read it in a book. So there are different ways we can learn. Maybe we believe without any reasoning at all.

Just because we have a certain idea, does not make it the truth or a fact. On the other hand, the fact that we do not believe an idea does not make it wrong or mistaken. Could it be that the facts we find could make the idea right or wrong? It is easy to believe we should follow the facts in making our decisions. This would apply to any subject we might study in an effort to find the truth about that particular subject. So in order to find the correct answers we must consider the information with an open mind. Then, to be fair with ourselves, we must accept the truth as we find it. If we find ideas about religion that are hard to believe, that is all right. Sometimes reason and facts prove we had accepted mistaken ideas in the beginning. After we learn the truth, we can really believe and accept the truth with full confidence. It is then easy to give up the mistaken idea. So it is necessary to have an open mind in our study about religion. The beliefs accepted must be based on reason and facts.

MUST WE UNDERSTAND AND SEPARATE FACTS FROM IDEAS?

It is reasonable to tell ourselves that an idea does not have to be a fact. People used to believe the earth was flat, but that idea was found to be a mistake. The truth is that the earth is round.

A person might have an idea that he could be a lawyer. To make this a fact he would have to study law and then pass his examinations. Next, he would have to pass the state bar examinations in order to practice law in his state. Then he would be a lawyer. That would make it a fact. Certain people held to the idea that human beings could get to the moon in space ships or rockets. At this time, since this feat has actually been accomplished, it is no longer an idea, it is a fact.

Some facts are easy to believe. It is easy to believe that the sun heats the air around us. It is easy to believe that rainstorms provide us with the water we need to live on the earth.

Other facts are harder to believe. It is hard to believe that people can die from eating too much food. However, doctors will tell us this is a fact. It is hard to believe that most of the people on earth could be killed by atomic bombs. Still, leading authorities in this field, will tell you it probably is true.

So in religon, as in mathematics, science, medicine, and other fields, we must separate ideas from the truth or the facts. If we must follow reasoning and the truth in everyday living; then certainly we must seek the truth in finding God and believing in Him so we can prepare for life after death. We must earn God's everlasting reward by serving Him as best we can. One very important fact to remember is that the length of time a human being lives on earth is very uncertain. No person knows how long he will live here. Are we being fair with ourselves if we spend all our efforts on earthly things that we might have to give up any day or hour? Death is absolutely inevitable for every creature on the earth. That is one of God's most important laws for people.

ARE THE IDEAS ABOUT RELIGION COMPLICATED?

If God is going to be fair and just with His human beings, does it seem likely that He would want the ideas about religion to be complicated and difficult for people to understand? It seems reasonable to assume God does not want it that way.

Let us analyze the conditions as we find them. The ideas or thoughts about religion, as you would normally use the term religion, are so complicated that by the time you have talked about it with other people, you usually end up by not getting much out of it. So most people would finally say: "Let every person believe and practice religion in any way he wants to." This seems to be an easy out for many people. Thus, they don't have to be afraid of offending the pride of another human being. This also avoids disagreement on what they should believe and do for their individual religious duties. Of course this amounts to putting the question of religious beliefs back on the shelf, so to speak.

This does not answer the question for any person who would really like to know what his religious duties to God would consist of. So in order to find the truth we must continue our search.

It is very apparent that religious beliefs and practices all over the world present a very complicated and confusing situation for a person interested in serving God. This complicated condition, which is due to the many different religious beliefs, is brought to light by the very fact there are such a great number of different churches and religious sects in the world today. Could we reason it out that there must be considerable confusion in the minds of people about religion? I believe the great number of different religious organizations existing today would be very good proof of the confusion in the minds of people all over the world. This widespread agreement to disagree about how to serve God certainly doesn't solve the problem and we must go further in our search.

IS A PERSON ABLE TO CHOOSE
HIS OWN PLAN FOR RELIGION?

If we said that every person should worship God as he pleases, how would that work out? Supposing you were to decide for yourself what your religious beliefs and practices should be. You could have your own religion, and every other person would have the same right to do this. I am afraid the confusion in religion would grow by leaps and bounds. Thus our intelligence tells us that this is not a very good plan.

How would a person know the best way to worship God? First, I believe we can assume that many people do not know what is best for them to do in minor, everyday decisions they have to make. If we do not know best about things we are in contact with from day to day, then how can we understand the best way to serve God in religion? If we cannot understand earthly things, then how can we decide what is best for us in supernatural affairs?

It seems logical that God would know just exactly how He

would expect His own creatures to serve Him. So it is not hard to believe that people are not capable of determining the best way to serve God. It seems reasonable to believe that God would have His own plans for His creatures rather than the creatures planning for God. Because God has created all human beings and has complete control over everything, He alone knows what is best for human beings to do to serve Him. Again we should remember that a person uses his free will in accepting or fighting what God has already planned for him. So we can accept the fact that God's plans are best for all of us.

ARE HUMAN BEINGS CREATED BY A SUPERNATURAL CREATOR?

This question has been discussed at great length and for a long time by human beings. It seems reasonable to assume that God doesn't have to pass on to human beings the knowledge of how the first people were created and placed on this earth. Maybe God doesn't expect us to understand what really happened at that time. God created our first parents at the time He chose for Himself. Also He created them in the manner He alone desired; at least no human being had anything to do with it. That makes it easy to understand that God created people just exactly as He wanted them. The conditions that we face in living on earth were all planned by God.

It is easy to believe that every person of average intelligence realizes some time during his life that a very powerful Creator made the world and all of its inhabitants. The whole universe is included in God's creations.

Since we are not supernatural beings, we cannot understand how God can create, apparently from nothing, anything He wants and then endow it with life. Every human being is a living proof of God's creative power. How a person was created is not too important to the individual. Most important to him is what a person actually does during his lifetime to prepare for life after death. The fact remains we are here on earth as living creatures of God, in the manner God had planned. The present civilization that has been built up in most parts of the world is outstanding proof of the unbelievable accomplishments of weak human beings. Just think of all the things that have been done by little creatures of God! What God is like is absolutely beyond the greatest powers of imagination or intelligence of any human being.

DID GOD CREATE PEOPLE SO THEY KNOW EXACTLY HOW TO SERVE HIM?

Supposing God had created each one of us so that we knew absolutely for sure what our religious obligations were to Him. Do you think God would have any further obligation to let us know what He expected from us? It seems reasonable that He would not need to do anything further to help us. Also God, in His justice, would give each one of us the power and strength to serve Him properly without any help from Him. We would be able to follow God's wishes without any difficulty. Of course we know from experience that this is not the way human beings are made.

So God did not create us with the knowledge and strength to serve Him exactly as He desires. Therefore, it is up to us to try to serve God the best way we can while living on earth. Again, we can remember that our conscience and our reasoning power are two very important guides that God has given us to help us live to please Him. We must accept the events in our life that we cannot change. Thus we are accepting the will of God and trying to serve Him. God wants us to have faith in Him even though we cannot see Him.

DID GOD CREATE MAN WITH AN INSTINCT TO
WORSHIP HIM AS A SUPERNATURAL BEING?

In all written history there is much proof that people have always worshipped a supernatural being of one kind or another. In their ignorance, they could imagine all types of supernatural creatures that seemed to influence their lives. They apparently understood that some unseen power had control over everything on earth.

This would prove to me that mankind was created with an instinct for or the ability to worship a Supreme Creator. In some way or other God has created in each normal human being an instinct or conscience that tells them they are subject to a creator they do not know. If God had not made people with the ability and the urge to worship a Supreme Being, how could He expect His weak and ignorant creatures to turn to Him for help? Thus it is reasonable to say that God does give man the ability to worship Him as a supernatural Being.

CAN HUMAN BEINGS WORSHIP
OTHER HUMAN BEINGS?

It is easy to check our own experiences and recall a person or persons who had great respect for another person. To a certain degree, they worshipped this individual. There are many examples of children who worship their father or mother or both parents to quite a degree. Now if children can worship their parents, certainly we are created so that we can worship God Himself to a much greater degree.

We can seek the help of God in spite of our human weaknesses and faults. God accepts us as we are. He certainly couldn't wait for us to become perfect human beings. We wouldn't even need His help if we were perfect. So He is always ready to help the weak little people He has created. Since God wanted people weak and ignorant, He certainly can't condemn and punish them for being what He wanted.

It certainly must be pleasing to God to have people love and respect each other.

DOES GOD CREATE PEOPLE WITH THE ABILITY TO SERVE OTHER HUMAN BEINGS?

We know that people can serve each other right here on this earth. Many people have been servants to leaders of governments. Any person holding a public office is considered to be a public servant, serving the interests of all the people. Kings have had many servants to help them. Children serve their parents and obey their wishes.

However, human beings are capable of helping each other only in a limited way. The more serious the problem an individual faces the harder it becomes for another person to help him. Maybe one person can't help another who is dying, but he can give the sick person consolation by trying to help him understand that God knows what is best for all of us. We can put our trust in God at all times. So there are many ways people can serve other human beings.

CAN HUMAN BEINGS SERVE TWO MASTERS?

It is not hard to believe that a person cannot serve more than one master. If God wants us to ask Him for help and then depend on Him, it seems certain He would create each one of us so that we will do best when serving Him alone. Thus, serving one master is the answer to that problem.

It is very difficult for a person to serve two or more people in authority during the same period of time. One master will want him to do one thing and the other master will tell him something different. He can't obey both of them, so he must either do nothing at all or he must choose which one he will obey. I believe it is that way with God. A person either has to try to do what he feels God or Jesus would want or else decide to do what human beings want him to do. Of course, if there seems to be a conflict with what a person believes God wants and what human beings demand, then the person should ignore what the human being wants. Our reasoning tells us to follow what we feel God would want.

Sometimes another person would suggest the same that we ourselves feel is in accordance with what God would want us to do. Then there is no conflict. This is where our reasoning and conscience would help us decide what God would like. In that case the individual is still serving only one master, because God comes first. The other person is merely in agreement with the will of God.

DO WE HAVE TO SERVE GOD IN ALL THINGS?

No. It doesn't seem reasonable that anyone is forced to serve God in all things. We can find plenty of examples of ways a person can serve other people in everyday living.

Even earthly things attract people so strongly that they really become slaves to one particular thing or another. They might become so obsessed with making money that they would ruin their health for just a little more of it. Other human beings become less important to them than the money they can make.

Human beings may want so much material wealth for themselves that they don't think about other people. They become self-centered. These people are very apt to forget about God and their real purpose for being on earth.

Children can avoid serving their parents if they try hard enough to get out of obeying them. To a certain extent they can try to do just as they please. We don't have to obey people who have authority over us, but a person can't expect to get along very well if he doesn't try to cooperate with other people. If it is important for us to try to cooperate with other people, how very important it becomes to try to cooperate with God Himself.

Because of our free will, God gives us the ability to choose whether or not we want to serve Him. We don't have to try to serve God, but we still have to go on living the best way we can without His help; that is, the supernatural help He is so willing to give everyone.

Most of us realize the value of a real close and faithful friend. This is the type of person who will help us when we are in need. They won't forget us. If a good friend can help us, just think how much more Christ Himself can help us.

How can we cooperate with God when we can't see or hear Him? Well, we can submit our will to what God allows to happen to us. Then we are going along with the things God allows to happen. Since God certainly does have control over the earth and every human being here, a person might just as well accept the fact he is helpless and at the mercy of God. That is just good judgment on the part of the individual.

DID GOD CREATE HUMAN BEINGS JUST AS HE WANTED THEM TO BE?

Since God does have absolute control over the creation of all human beings through the laws of nature, it is easy to believe that every human being is just exactly as God wanted him to be. Parents have no way of choosing whether their child will be a boy or a girl. God does the choosing through nature. What about the physical characteristics of a child? No one knows for sure what a child will be like. These things are very important to the child and have great influences on its life. Still, the child has no choice of his own.

Why are babies so weak and helpless? Through nature, God has already planned the way He wanted babies to be. God places these children under the care and guidance of weak human beings, their parents or other people responsible for raising them. That is His plan. He knows that mistakes will be made in this training of children. Since God allows it to be this way, why should we feel that we have any right to question God's plan for His creatures?

We must recognize the fact that all the weaknesses of human beings can be passed down from one generation to another, from parents to children. Even as children grow up, they imitate and learn from other people they come in contact with. What they learn may help them or it may hurt their characters. We are all more or less influenced by the people around us. Even though we know people grow up in these surroundings and are subject to the mistakes and weaknesses of other human beings, we still can remember that God planned it exactly that way. God loves each one of His creatures, and because He does not make mistakes, we can trust Him and understand this is the best way for beings to live. Even if we can't understand it, no human being can change these things.

DID GOD CREATE THE WORLD AS HE WANTED IT?

Whatever way the world was created, it certainly seems reasonable to believe that God did cause it to be made just exactly as He wanted it to be.

In almost any place around the world we care to look we can see the beauty of nature. Witness the mountains with their peaks of such tremendous size and height or the canyons—many of them so deep we can hardly see the bottom. All of these earthly creations of God only help prove to us the power of God in making all these things. Also, we humans are so little and insignificant in size compared with many of these wonders of nature, it makes us feel pretty small and helpless.

The earth and all these conditions are part of the plan of God. All people are subject to God's laws of nature. One of the natural laws is that all living things on earth shall be replaced by others newborn and then they, too, will finally die. All people die—some young, some old. Human beings all struggle one way or another to survive and live here. The earth is a proving ground for human beings. Those who try to follow what God has planned for them will be rewarded by our Creator Himself.

People rule the earth as far as animals and other living creatures are concerned; that is, with the exception of those creatures that live so deep in the oceans that they are out of reach of human beings. As man dominates the earth, so God dominates man and everything else He has created.

DOES THE SUPERNATURAL POWER OF GOD HELP TO PROVE THE WEAKNESS AND HELPLESSNESS OF HIS CREATURES?

It certainly is not hard to believe that God does have complete power over every human being. There is nothing any human being can do to change this control of God over mankind. Man has no power at all to make anything and then put life into it. Reason tells us that most of God's power over people is taken care of through His laws of nature, and these cannot be changed. People can only go so far in helping themselves or others in sickness, poverty, mental ills, and other suffering they are subject to. Beyond this help, nature is in control of human beings. We are all certainly weak and helpless in the face of tornadoes, floods, storms at sea, rain, and other forces of nature.

God first created the earth and the rest of the universe in the manner He wanted to. Since that time He has kept order in the universe according to His plan. When we think of all the creations of God, it is easily understood that human beings are very insignificant.

WHY DID GOD CREATE HUMAN BEINGS SO WEAK AND HELPLESS AND YET SO INTELLIGENT?

It is not hard to understand that people are weak in many different ways. Each person is weak in one way or another. We all have our faults as a result of our human nature. People are helpless at different times and in many different ways. Our intelligence can be used to help us find ways to do things for ourselves. Many times we are thinking about helping other people.

Through our intelligence we can understand that there are so many things God has done that we as human beings absolutely cannot have power such as God possesses. We can understand that because of our weakness, our only real help is to turn to God.

With our free will we turn to God for help. If we are sincere in having faith in God, He will either take away our trouble, or He will console us and give us courage to carry on. This is God's way of proving to people that we all need His help.

Since God loves His creatures as only their Creator can, He must give them good reasons to come to Him for help. Therefore, it is necessary for human beings to have trials and troubles to practically drive them to God for help. They are urged on by the trials and tribulations of life on earth. Through these events we can learn to look forward to a completely happy life in heaven.

If we could only feel that we are simple, ignorant servants of an unseen King, it would be much easier for us to bear our trials. God is a supernatural King Who is all-loving, all-kind, all-forgiving and Whom we must try to serve to the best of our ability. All faithful servants will be gloriously rewarded by God our King.

Thus we can understand that the purpose of God in creating people so weak and helpless, and yet so intelligent, was to help us to learn to ask Him for help.

WHY WAS THE HUMAN RACE PLACED ON EARTH TO LIVE UNDER THE CONDITIONS THAT EXIST HERE?

It is reasonable to believe that God has definite plans for His creatures living on earth. We can, therefore, assume that God has made the conditions on earth just exactly as they should be. These conditions are the very best for people if they are recognized as a means for serving God. We can understand that God has made man to live to serve Him, not to serve the whims of our weak human nature.

If we are going to be able to earn a place in Heaven with God, we must be placed where we can work for it. God, in His justice, allows us to be born on earth. That is our chance to live and work to serve God. He certainly is pleased to have us pray to Him for help to guide us and consolation to help us bear our suffering. When God consoles us during our trials and sufferings, we can understand this is our way to earn our everlasting reward in heaven.

When we live to serve and please ourselves, all our trials and sufferings on earth seem to hurt us. They keep us from getting what we want for ourselves. We get discouraged and our trials seem worse than before. Our efforts seem to be in vain.

When we try to serve God, our sufferings take on a new meaning. We have something to offer up to God. We remember how much Christ suffered at the hands of ignorant human beings. He offered His sufferings up to God in Heaven. If Christ had to suffer because of human beings, how can we expect not to have trials and troubles? Also, our reason tells us we could not offer up earthly pleasures, and satisfactions to God. That is something we get temporary pleasure out of; we are not earning anything.

It seems so easy for those people who have the slightest troubles to complain. Many people with the greatest troubles complain the least. Could it be that this ability to bear sufferings and trials is the result of the person's faith and trust in Christ or God? I believe it is. We know that a mother can make a child feel much better by loving and consoling it when it is suffering. It certainly is the child's faith and trust in its mother that helps so much when suffering comes. God or Christ can comfort people with a supernatural love and understanding.

God has created things on earth, and we have to work and suffer and give up other things so we can gain the thing we are trying to accomplish right here on earth. Anything that is worthwhile in life we have to earn one way or another. So, certainly, we have to earn any heavenly reward from God the same way— by suffering, work, and self-denial.

WHAT ABOUT ADAM AND EVE?

This is a question that probably has caused confusion in the minds of many people—religious leaders and others.

How can we approach this scene, which had to happen or we wouldn't be here? Someone had to be the first man and someone else had to be the first woman.

Just how did God create Adam and Eve? It seems reasonable to believe that no human being knows exactly what happened at that time. It is not important for us to know about this, only to understand how we are affected through our first parents. The manner of creation is not important. What is of great importance is the human characteristics that Adam and Eve passed on to all their descendants. It just doesn't seem reasonable that human nature has changed to any noticeable degree since Adam and Eve. Certainly, as a child grows up it acts and thinks in the manner to which it has been trained. As a child grows into an adult, he or she begins to reason more independently. However, the childhood training is of very great importance during the life of the person.

Through our own human nature and that of our parents or other people, we can understand a little what Adam and Eve must have been like. If we are like them, they were like we are. The result would be that as adult people, Adam and Eve would be very similar to a man and a woman we would see any place today. The differences probably would be that Adam and Eve did not have any clothes, or tools, or anything to work with.

God, in His love and justice, would provide the means for His first man and woman to get their food, clothing, and shelter. This they could do with their intelligence, reasoning, eyes, hands, and feet. God made them just exactly as they should be to live on this earth. Probably God arranged it so that the climate was warm enough and they didn't suffer from lack of shelter. It also seems reasonable that fruit or vegetables ready for them to eat were easily found. People can move from one place to another if necessary to get food, shelter, and other things needed for them to live. It is easy to believe the first parents lived a very simple life. Apparently, God's plan was to put Adam and Eve on earth and provide everything necessary for them to live and survive long enough to raise children and start the human race we have today. How long they lived we can only guess, but they did live long enough for the plan of God to be fulfilled.

It is reasonable to believe that Adam and Eve had time to think about how they came to be living on this earth. Their reasoning could tell them a supernatural Being had to make them in some way not known to them. They probably worshipped Him the best way they could. Through their human ignorance and imagination, they could have learned to fear an unknown God. Today, God doesn't appear to people and tell them what to do or not to do. Why should He have to appear to Adam and Eve to tell them how to live? Reason tell us God has already created His creatures in such a way that they are able to take care of themselves on earth, if they think and live in the manner He has planned for them. If they follow the laws of nature the best way they know how, and have faith in God helping them, people will be living according to God's plan. Just how Adam and Eve should have served God and loved Him is probably unknown to human beings of this age. We don't really know what information they had about God. Since we all have our own souls to save, serving God is a problem to be solved by each individual for himself.

It seems reasonable to believe that the importance of Adam and Eve to the people living today lies in the fact that we have inherited our human characteristics from them down through the generations. Thus, we are like them just as God planned it so long ago.

Since God loves His creatures with a supernatural love, our intelligence tells us, or allows us to understand, that anyone who ever saw God or felt His presence would not run away from Him in fear and terror. In fact, we just can't run away from God. God's love for us will draw us to Him if we believe and trust in Him. Regardless of how much we fear God, there is absolutely no place a human being can go to get away from the power of God.

If human beings do not know about God only from what they see in nature, they might fear God through ignorance. Ignorance causes fear, and fear causes hate. When a human being hates God, he doesn't even want to try to follow God's will or try to serve Him. This person wants to stay away from God.

So it seems reasonable to conclude that Adam and Eve were people very much like we are with all the God-given weaknesses and ignorance of other human beings. Remember, God created them just exactly as He wanted them. If God is pleased with His own creatures why should we condemn any of them?

WERE ADAM AND EVE FREE TO CHOOSE
WHAT THEY WANTED TO DO?

It would seem that they were as free as any human beings could be to go about and do as they pleased. They were limited by the laws of nature, just as all human beings are for all time until God changes it.

They had to make use of earthly things found by them, and they had to live the best way they could. It would be easy to picture in our minds Adam and Eve roaming around in the surroundings in which they found themselves, wondering what the reason was for their existence here on earth. Through their free will, they were able to decide what to try to do or not to do.

Whatever the obligations were that they felt they had toward God we do not know, and I don't think we ever will know. These are things important to God but not to all mankind. God, because He created them, understood the ignorance and weaknesses of humankind. They were just exactly as He had planned them to be. God, in His mercy and compassion, must have looked down upon them with great love and forgiveness. He still had to let Adam and Eve make the mistakes that all human beings are apt to make. The reason was that God had given them free will.

A good mother does not let her child go outdoors and play and then punish it very severely when the child falls down and gets hurt. The good mother will take the child up in her arms and love it. She will comfort her child and tell it everything will be all right. The mother will teach her child the right way to play without getting hurt. In other words she will help the child instead of punishing and abusing it, thus driving it away from her. Certainly we can expect God to do a much better job of helping His weak creatures. Our reasoning tells God will not abuse and punish us when we are in trouble and need His help. He will love and comfort us.

We certainly can believe that Adam and Eve were free to

choose what they wanted to do within the laws of nature. Whether they understood enough about God to ask Him for help or not, I don't believe human beings can determine a correct answer.

WHY HAS GOD ALLOWED HUMAN BEINGS TO TREAT EACH OTHER AS THEY HAVE SINCE OUR FIRST PARENTS?

It is easy to believe that God should some way or other interfere when human beings go so far as to injure and even kill each other. As we search for an answer we must consider that God gives each one the free will to decide for himself what to do. That is the reason He does not interfere with the actions of human beings directly by forcing them to do what might seem to be His will, human beings just never know for sure what purpose God has in allowing those things to happen. Many times innocent people suffer from the acts of other persons who have fear and hatred in their hearts. Many times vicious people are greatly surprised by the way these persons, who place their trust in God, are able to take abuse and suffering. Thus, they begin to realize the courage God can give to His weak creatures. The murder of Christ is the greatest example of suffering endured by any human being to help other people. Christ possessed both human and divine natures. Every human being has to suffer one way or another in order to earn his reward from God after death.

What are people to do when other human beings endanger their health and even their lives? Our human instinct is to fight back and defend ourselves. Our reasoning and conscience could tell us to depend absolutely on God for help to survive. When a person is completely helpless, his only chance is to ask God to save him. Most people in that situation will call on God for help.

If God should force people to stop fighting each other and doing other things to hurt each other, He would be taking from them their free will. God gives everyone free will and He must allow them to use it as they desire. However, He does not interfere with some human beings forcing others to submit to them. That is usually the way people or nations rule each other, by physical force. They can submit willfully instead of fighting if they want to.

It seems reasonable to believe that people live as they do mainly because of the human characteristics God has created in their minds and hearts. The human instinct to follow other people is very strong. Because God already knows and understands His creatures perfectly, I don't think He gets very excited about what they do.

The important thing to God is the ability of the person to turn to Him for help and consolation in trials and suffering. So it is entirely up to the individual to ask God for help the best way he can.

SHOULD GOD FORCE HUMAN BEINGS TO FOLLOW HIS WILL AND LIVE TO SERVE HIM?

God could certainly do this if He desired it. If this was the plan God followed, each human being would have to do what God wanted without any choice at all. Therefore, he would not be earning any reward God might have for him after death. If all students in school were absolutely forced to study in order to be graduated from college and be successful in their life work, there would not be any sense to a reward for hard work due to their own free will. It just wouldn't work that way.

So it is with human beings earning any reward from God after death. All God can do is prove to us that we all will live for a while and that, in due time, we all will die. God will give His reward according to the way we have tried to serve Him.

Other human beings can do very little to help us; after death they can do nothing.

God does have complete control of every human being. Most of this control is through God's laws of nature. Man has no choice about the results of not following the laws of nature. He can train himself to put off thinking about death, but sooner or later he will die in spite of anything a human being can do about it. This power of God still does not change a man's free will to choose whether he will try to follow God's will and laws or not. He can still fight what God does but he can't do anything about it.

DID GOD HAVE DEFINITE PLANS FOR THE HUMAN RACE AFTER ADAM AND EVE?

I believe that very little is known about what God really expected from His creatures at the time of the creation of Adam and Eve. After having made them so helpless and ignorant, God couldn't expect very much from them. Due to their very basic characteristics, designed by God Himself, human beings are very apt to make errors in judgment about God, and they are naturally not able to fulfill promises they make to themselves and others. They just don't have enough will power to carry out their plans. Knowing all these facts about His own creatures, God understands better than any human being, how He must deal with them. That is the reason why God does not condemn and viciously punish His little people. God's supernatural love and compassion and forgiveness are the only things that will draw His creatures to Him. Through their free will they can ask Him for His help and guidance.

It seems easy to understand that the conscience God has built into the minds of people has been used by them to help them realize they were created by a supernatural power. Their reasoning power told them God was all powerful and had them under His control. Their conscience was a very good guide to help them feel they had done something to please God. Their conscience also could make them feel discouraged if they had done something they thought was wrong. However, they could have been disturbed by fear and ignorance about God, and then they wouldn't know whether they had done anything wrong or not.

It is not natural for people to run away from anything they understand and know. But it is human nature for people to fear and to run in panic from something they don't understand and that scares them. This makes it easy to believe that the first people did not know about God in heaven any more than we do today. So the storms and other forces of nature must have been terrifying to our ancestors. It would be easy for them to believe God was angry with them when they became ill or injured, or their crops failed to grow. Then they could not understand why God allowed those things to happen. They probably could not understand what they had done to displease God. This may help us understand why they made offerings to an unknown God. They were attempting to appease His anger. That is what they thought in their ignorance and lack of knowledge of God. It seemed as though God was punishing them for things they did not understand. By this time their imagination could let them believe God was very severe in His punishment of them. Eventually, in their ignorance about God many gradually fell away from trying to follow Him. The natural instincts of human beings to follow other people and to believe in them probably influenced many people in their way of living. It also would affect their thinking about God, their unknown creator.

The one bright ray of hope that seemed to come from God to earth was the feeling or premonition that God would send a Redeemer from heaven to help the human race. Those people who had faith in God were the ones who felt this was the help God would give them. Very probably, those who had lost faith or confidence in God were the people who turned to pagan gods. They might even worship animals or figures they made themselves. This is just an example of what happens when people try to decide for themselves how to live and how to worship. There were a few people, called prophets, who seemed to understand that God would sometime send someone to redeem the human race. Apparently, God's plan was to let a few people understand that He would send someone to help the human race. When would this time come? That was probably something no one knew. We can assume God knew the proper time the human race was ready for the Redeemer He was going to send. Maybe God waited until people understood the fact that they were greatly in need of help from Him. They gradually realized no human being could give the help that was needed so much.

Since God is the Master of all creation, it seems reasonable to believe that He had planned everything in advance just as He wanted it to be. Thus, God planned the coming of Christ on earth at the time He desired to help the human race. Christ certainly came on earth at a time when people were greatly confused about the kind of a god they should worship and the way they should live.

WHAT WAS GOD'S PURPOSE IN SENDING CHRIST ON EARTH?

It certainly seems that the only purpose of God's sending Christ on earth was to help the human race. How could Christ give the people the help they needed so badly. In the first place He could reassure them that God in Heaven loved His creatures instead of hating them. Christ told His followers to follow the will of His Father in Heaven. They were advised by Christ to turn away from the things of the earth and live to prepare for a life in Heaven with God.

There were many people who believed God was very vicious with His creatures. People also believed God would deliberately punish weak human beings by floods, sickness, and all types of tragedies if He was angry about things they did. Could He be so cruel as to make them burn forever after death in eternal flames? To overcome these mistaken ideas about God, Christ was to tell the people that God loved His creatures with an ever-lasting love. Love your neighbor, Christ told them. Forgive your neighbor when he does wrong, He reminded them. Help each other instead of harming anyone. Thus Christ, by His words, brought new knowledge to the minds of His followers about the love of God in Heaven for His weak creatures. He told them things God wanted them to do while living on earth.

Thus we find Christ on earth, as a representative of God, to teach the people how they should learn to depend on God instead of human beings for help. He told them how to treat their fellow human beings. Christ told them to love and help their neighbors instead of harming them. If God doesn't want us to harm our neighbors, He certainly has no plans to harm them Himself.

HOW DID CHRIST LIVE WHILE ON EARTH?

The life of Christ on earth is much better covered by writers of history and religion than we can do in these few pages. His life here on earth has left such an impact on the human race that time is recorded before and after His birth. Christmas is the most important time of year. Even though it is very commercialized, most people still realize it commemorates the birth of Christ. Next in importance is Easter Sunday, along with Holy Week before Easter. Most people still realize Easter Sunday represents the resurrection of Christ three days after His death on the Cross. Thus, we understand how these events of 2000 years ago are still remembered as the most important days of the year. Most important was the establishment of Christianity as the result of Christ's life, death, and resurrection from death, while on earth.

In these pages we will consider some of the most important

events of Christ's life on earth. What did Jesus do or say that is important to people living today?

Christ was born in a stable that was used as a shelter for animals. Mary and Joseph had sought a place to stay for the night but could not find any. So, according to God's plan, Christ was born in a stable. This places His coming on earth in the lowest and most humble position possible. God chose to let the simple shepherds know about the Christ Child and guided them to the stable so that they could worship Him. We are told about the Wise Men who followed the star of Bethlehem to find Jesus in the manger. This was the beginning of a very humble and simple life on earth for Christ. He was without the material things of the earth that so many people fight so hard to get and work so hard to keep. Why did Jesus live in such poverty and live such a simple life? One reason was that He told the people not to put their faith and trust in earthly things. So Christ was a great example to them by living the way He told them to live. People just can't be both slaves to materialism and live to serve God at the same time. The way Christ lived could help prove to people that even the poorest and the simplest human beings are pleasing and acceptable to God in Heaven.

It is not hard to understand that people who want so many material possessions just don't have time to think much about God Himself. So, very slowly but surely, they drift away from God and stop trying to serve Him. They cannot serve two masters. Material things being one master and God the Creator, the other.

Jesus was a friend to the poor people and to those who were considered as outcasts. Through the miracles He performed at different times, Christ proved His Supernatural power. His miracles also showed His love and great concern for those who had faith in Him, proving that supernatural help is available to people here on earth who have Faith in God and Christ.

The miracle of the loaves and fishes that fed about 5000 people was an example of Christ's great powers, and still he was a human being. After feeding the people, He told them He wanted to give them His Body and His Blood so they could have

life everlasting. He could only mean He wanted to give Himself
to them to help them. This they could not understand, so they
turned and left Him. They were only interested in the material
gifts He might give them. Of course Christ had no earthly
things to give to them.

There had been talk among the people about God sending
a Redeemer to earth. They didn't know what He would be like.
It isn't hard to believe that people would expect Christ to come
to earth in great pomp and glory. As a young man, Christ left
His home and went out among the people. He was so humble
and lived such a simple life that it was hard for people to believe He was actually Christ sent by God.

If Christ was to redeem human beings, how would He do
it? Maybe "redeemer" is not quite the right word to use. It
seems reasonable to believe Christ was on earth to teach people
about God in Heaven. He told them of God's love, compassion,
and forgiveness for His weak creatures on earth. What the people believed and how they lived after hearing Christ was entirely up to them. They decided for themselves through their
own free will. Christ could not help people unless they really
wanted His help and would accept His teachings. The fact that
Christ lived and died on earth did not change the way people
in general lived.

We must reason deeper. Christ had a very definite mission
on earth to do something for all the people from that time on.
Otherwise His life on earth would directly affect only the few
people He actually came in contact with at that time. Christ's
teaching about the goodness of God to His creatures was information that one generation could pass on to the next one. People
needed more direct help than that. Their weak human natures
required supernatural help. That is one reason why Christ told
the people He was here to do the will of His Father in Heaven.
There were numerous times when Christ told His apostles it
was the faith in God and in Christ Himself that was so important
to human beings.

We must live on earth without having any absolute knowledge about living in heaven with God. It is this ability of weak

human beings to blindly follow God's will that is so remarkable. It certainly proves faith in God when people live their lives without actually knowing what their destiny will be after death. Still, they follow God blindly the best way they can. We must remember that Christ and God will always give people who sincerely ask for it the help they need. This supernatural help will solve their problems or will give them courage and strength to bear their burdens and thus strengthen their faith in God and Christ. God just couldn't love people and refuse to help them. God is not angry with His creatures, and He is not vicious with them.

Another very important part of Christ's life on earth was His passion and death, followed by His resurrection. Christ had already told His followers He would be killed and in three days He would rise up from the dead. It was natural for them to doubt that He could come back to life again after death.

Christ died as a human being and then was resurrected as a supernatural being. This helps to prove the existence of life after death for human beings. Reason tells us human beings can prove for themselves very little about the fate of souls after death. That is a mystery very well kept for God Himself to know.

The passion and death on the Cross of Christ was of great importance to people in helping them to understand He was actually sent by God to help them. First He was crucified on the Cross as a blasphemer simply because He would not deny that He was the Son of God. For a person to suffer the punishment that Christ suffered was not the fate of an ordinary person. All He had to do was tell Pilate He was not the Son of God. Then He would have been spared the suffering and death on the Cross. Christ could not tell them He was not sent by God to help the human race. Therefore, He died rather than lie to them. The way He died was a terrific shock to those who witnessed the execution. Christ called on God in Heaven to forgive those who murdered Him, because they knew not what they were doing, murdering the Son of God. This was a most important example to all human beings of the faith Christ had in God. His faith carried Christ through all the trials and sufferings He had to endure on earth. Thus, Christ was such a wonderful example of one who practiced what He preached. Love and forgiveness for the very people who were murdering Him on the Cross were shown by Christ while He was dying, hanging on the Cross. At this time a number of vicious unbelievers were converted to believing Christ was actually the Son of God. They later became some of the first martyrs because they could no longer deny Christ.

WHAT WAS THE PURPOSE OF THE LAST SUPPER?

There are different versions or beliefs about the real purpose of Christ in assembling the Apostles at the Last Supper.

Let us reason it through in the simplest way. Christ had already told His followers: "I want to give you My Body and My Blood, that you may have eternal life."

At the Last Supper, Christ had the chalice and again said in pouring the wine "This is My Blood." In breaking the bread, He said "This is My Body." This is what Christ really meant when He said it. Would He have any reason to deceive the Apostles or anyone else about what He meant to do at the Last Supper? I don't believe we can assume Christ meant anything else but what He said.

The purpose of the Last Supper was for Christ to give His Body and Blood in a supernatural manner to any human being who wished to receive it. The Apostles were to carry on for Christ in presenting Christ's Body and Blood to those who believed and wanted His help.

It could seem as though Christ's mission on earth had been a definite failure. There were not many who were converted to complete faith and belief in Christ during His life. How then could Christ become important to Christians after His death, resurrection, and ascension into heaven? If He no longer existed on earth in any way, shape, or form, how could He have any definite influence on human beings? Many times while on earth Christ told the people to seek the help of "My Father in Heaven." Also, He told them, "I am here to do the will of My Father." God sent Christ on earth to help the human race. There could be no other important reason for Christ's mission on earth. If Christ no longer existed on earth, doesn't it seem very probable that people would gradually forget Christ and return to the same way of living as before He came? Most of the civilized world have accepted God as our creator and do not worship idols as they did before Christ. We can, therefore, believe that the effect of Christianity has been to teach many nations about God and a future life in God, in His great mercy and love for His weak human creatures, placed Christ on earth to help them.

HOW COULD CHRIST HELP PEOPLE
AFTER HIS ASCENSION INTO HEAVEN?

Since Christ was no longer on earth as a human being, there is no other answer except that He could exist on earth in a supernatural form or manner.

The accomplishments of Christ during His life on earth were the reasons for a new era in history, called Christianity. The Apostles, who were followers of Christ, formed a new religious organization. They were called Christians, or Followers of Christ.

The leaders of the Roman Empire were still determined to make the people forget about Christ. So they made a great effort to break up this small band of believers in Christ. Because of this, the Christians had to meet in secret to worship and practice their religion underground. There they received Holy Communion and prayed for help.

History tells us how the Romans would have great sport in forcing the Christians to go to the sports arenas and there be turned loose with man-eating lions that ran them down and killed them. The Christians had their choice: to deny and give up their faith in Christ, or to be thrown in with the lions. Usually, they refused to give up Christ and deny their belief in Him. Why would they rather die such a terrible death rather than give up Christ? How could they have the courage to let themselves be torn apart bodily and killed by the lions? Where was their human instinct to fight to live? Where was their pride when they were treated so cruelly by the Roman leaders? There is just one answer to all these questions. Those Christians were so greatly influenced by Christ Himself in a supernatural way that they could follow Him in spite of anything any other human being could do to force them to turn away from Him. Christ had been murdered on the Cross because He would not deny that He was the Son of God. Therefore, these Christians who died rather than deny their belief in Christ were truly followers of Christ.

When you try to compare human nature and human beings with supernatural beings and supernatural power, it is easy to see that there is absolutely no comparison. Man just cannot have any control over supernatural beings. while God has complete control and power over His creatures. As a result, any human being who believes and trusts in Christ or God is bound to receive the courage and strength to keep him a follower of Christ. Because of their unyielding faith in Christ, the early Christians influenced thousands of the pagans to become Christians and believe in Christ. Thus the influence of Christ Himself began to gradually spread to all parts of the world.

WHAT HAPPENED TO CAUSE CHANGES IN THE WAY EARLY CHRISTIANS LIVED AND THOSE OF SEVERAL CENTURIES LATER?

To begin with, early Christians followed the example set by Christ Himself. They lived simple lives, as Christ had done before them. They received Christ's Body and Blood in Holy Communion. They went directly to Christ for help and consolation. Christ gave them tremendous faith and courage because they believed and trusted Him. As we remember what happened to Christians when the Romans discovered them, we can understand that Christians worshipped and believed in Christ at the risk of their lives.

It is logical to believe that, as some church leaders became more powerful and influential among the people of different nations during the centuries following the time of Christ, they began to drift away from the ideals established by Christ. The weakness of human nature began to show itself among the leaders. Wealth and power, as a result of leading a more earthly life, began to bring changes in the reasoning of church leaders. The church laws and doctrines were determined by human beings. Thus these regulations were subject to the chance of human misunderstanding or errors by the church leaders.

Unless a person follows the example of Christ and the teachings of Christ, his life can be completely changed and he will follow the road of materialism. A very good example can be seen when a man is born and raised in a poor family. As a poor boy he leads a simple life and works hard for his meager possessions. His earthly fortunes improve and he finds himself a wealthy married man with a family. Now his humility changes to pride, his love for his neighbors changes to disgust and condemnation of poverty. He believes he is a much better person than other people who have fewer earthly possessions. He now feels he should domineer others around him. Materialism has become a deadly disease to his soul. His patience, happiness, and humility have vanished. His mind is now dominated by thinking about material possessions. He uses his wealth to get his way about things he wants to satisfy his earthly ambitions. We can see that he is a completely changed man. Poverty in his youth had been his best friend, but he didn't realize its true value after materialism overpowered his mind.

Thus it was with some of the church leaders. They gradually forgot about the great poverty of Christ on earth. Possession of church property and land and other forms of earthly wealth seemed to make the position of the church and its leaders more secure. Many leaders were sincere in their belief that earthly possessions would help the church survive and provide religious training with established practices from one generation to another. When we remember how the Christians at the time of Christ allowed themselves to be killed rather than give up their faith in Christ, we can understand they were following Christ Himself rather than depending on their own ideas and material wealth to promote the work of the church.

As human beings with power and wealth are apt to do, the church leaders had their arguments about what people could do or not do according to the laws and regulations of the church. A few broke away from the original church and formed new churches of their own. This was the period of the Reformation, a breaking away into different groups with different ideas about religion and serving God. If they had been following Christ Himself in the Blessed Sacrament, they would not have been fighting among themselves. Again we find an example of confusion in the minds of church leaders about how human beings should serve God through religion. We can understand how human beings change things when they decide to determine in their own way how they shall believe and what they shall practice in religion.

In previous pages we considered the fact that God knows what He wants people to believe and do. Since God is our Creator, He is our Master. We are weak, ignorant human servants. Therefore, we have no right to try to take God's or Christ's place on earth in determining religious practices and beliefs for other people. If our ideas are in agreement with the plans God has for His creatures, than we are right.

History has recorded the changes that have come about in the organization and doctrines of the various churches during the centuries since Christ lived on earth. There is no need to go into detail about these changes. That will not answer our problem about serving God.

Now we come to the place where we must analyze the situation human beings face today in their beliefs in God and

Christ. How can they serve God and how can they receive the help needed so badly?

In review we can feel that God will be just in His demands on human beings. Next we must be open-minded in finding Christ on earth. We need to use our conscience and our instinct to serve and worship God as our Creator. It must be remembered that we can serve only one master. Because He has given us freedom of will, God will not force us to turn to Him or Christ for help. So any effort to find Christ and receive His help must be through our own free will.

Just as the life and death of Christ on earth was the most important event in recorded history, so the sending of Christ to earth by God was the most important thing He has ever done to help people.

Part Two:

The Modern-Day Church

HOW CAN HUMAN BEINGS FIND CHRIST AND RECEIVE HIS SUPERNATURAL HELP AND GUIDANCE?

Now we have arrived at the most important question that can be discussed in our study of "Religion Through Reason." Can people really find Christ Himself present on earth in such a way that He will help them with their problems? Is He truly here after nearly 2000 years? Since we must ask Him for help, He is not going to run after any human being to give him help. Remember, God has turned us loose with our free will. Through our own choice we can seek Christ to receive His help.

We have already determined through reason and history that God sent His only Son Christ on earth nearly 2000 years ago to help the human race. The most important days of the year are in memory of Christ's life on earth. Christmas is Christ's birthday. Holy Week is the time of His suffering, death on the Cross, and burial. Easter Sunday is the day of the resurrection of Christ from death.

How can we discover where Christ is to be found on this earth? The most logical step to take is to go back to the time of Christ's life on earth. What did Christ say about Himself? He said "I have been sent by My Father in heaven to teach you and to help you. I want to give you My Body and My Blood." At the Last Supper, when He broke the bread and wine, Christ told the Apostles: "I give you My Body and My Blood." Thus the Blessed Sacrament was established on earth by Christ Himself. Reason tells us someone had to pass Christ's Body and Blood in the form of bread and wine to all the people who would come and receive it. The Apostles were the men Christ had chosen to do this for Him. They spread out and went to different parts of the world and established churches where people could go to Mass and receive Holy Communion. They were doing as Christ had instructed them to do.

Down through the centuries the Church has used the Mass and Holy Communion as the most important service in honoring

Christ. Today, Masses are being performed all over the world every day. Thus we can reason that Christ is to be found where He said He would be present, namely in the Blessed Sacrament.

If Christ is on earth in the supernatural form of the Blessed Sacrament, where can He be found? Many people believe Christ and God are everywhere on earth. It seems doubtful that Christ told people He would be everywhere on earth. I don't mean we can't pray to Christ anywhere we are. He wants us to pray to Him at any time, in any place. However, if Christ were everywhere, then there would be no need for the Blessed Sacrament. Then Christ would never have had the Last Supper. There would be no reason for it.

Why did Christ choose to be present in a supernatural form in the Blessed Sacrament? For Christ to be available to people all over the world, He must be present in a suitable form or manner. Suppose Christ was present in a form we could see, and suppose He was present in only twenty different places on earth. What would people think? Wouldn't they begin to say, Which one is the real Christ? Are any of these fakes just pretending to be Christ? Also, if Christ were present visibly, many thousands of people would come to see Him only out of curiosity, not to worship Him and ask for help. As Christ planned it, He is present in a supernatural form. We cannot actually see Him. However, He is present in the form of a small white Host, in such a small, humble, and insignificant manner that not many people realize He is there. No one is curious about such a small piece of unleavened bread. Thus, as Christ planned, those who seek Him in the Holy Eucharist, seek Him through faith and confidence, not through sight.

Those who seek Christ in a supernatural form on earth should look for the Blessed Eucharist or Host. Christ will be found in the church that is unlocked every day so that people may go inside. It is reasonable to believe Christ would plan it so that people could get inside the church when they wanted to come to Him for help. The next guide is a red sanctuary candle or lamp. This means the Holy Eucharist is present in the tabernacle. This is a small chest-like place in the center of the altar.

Since Christ had the Apostles establish the Catholic Church, that is where the Holy Eucharist is found at all times. When people are ready to ask Christ for help, there should be some place for them to go where He will be waiting for them in a supernatural way. There is so much noise and confusion in the outside world that people could not have the peace and quiet that is very essential to those who are in need of help. So God and Christ have arranged the place and the conditions under which we can go to Christ Himself to get His help.

Naturally, if people do not believe Christ is truly present in the Catholic church, they will not come to the church to visit Him. What if you can't understand that Christ is actually there to help you? People have to put enough faith in their doctor to go and seek his help. If we can depend on human beings to help us, why can't we just go and give Christ a chance to help us? We know for sure that human beings can never give us the help Christ can bestow on us. Since Christ loves all human beings, there is no person Christ will not help, unless a person would just pretend he believed in Christ and just went through the motions of faith in Christ. It is to be expected that Christ cannot reward a hypocrite or nonbeliever.

It is necessary to keep in mind that Christ is not a mere human being and that He does not deal with people in the same way people act toward each other. Regardless of the kind of life a person may have led up to the present, Christ will welcome him with the greatest love. Christ has the utmost compassion for the poor, discouraged, helpless creatures whom society has cast out with such viciousness and revenge. With Christ there are no favored people because of their wealth and social positions. To Him each person is a weak human being who needs so much the help Christ can give to him.

The real reason why people don't go to God or Christ for help is because they are getting along all right leading a materialistic life. They just haven't gone far enough down the road of life to meet with any serious obstacles. What can they do when they suddenly lose their jobs, their money, their health, their friends, their loved ones? That is the time they begin to realize, as the old saying goes, that all that glitters is not gold. What can they do when they just don't know where or how to get help? That is when discouragement, fear, and sickness of mind, heart, and body take over God's poor creatures. They will grasp for anything that will even give them temporary relief from this situation. Reasoning would tell us the time comes in all human lives when there is not one single thing on this earth that has any value to them; that is at the time of their death. Everything of a materialistic nature becomes worthless to them. They certainly cannot live for materialism and at the same time prepare for life after death with Christ and God. They just cannot serve two masters. However, these same people are the ones who are just not interested in finding Christ in the Blessed Sacrament in the Catholic church. They do not understand that every single human being needs the help of Christ every day he lives. They are apparently getting along all right as they are, but they know nothing about how soul-satisfying and beautiful and peaceful life can be under the guidance and help of Christ Himself.

Thus our reason can bring to us the faith and courage it takes for us to go to the Catholic churches where there is a peace and quiet that cannot be found any other place in the world. If Christ is supernaturally present there, shouldn't it be the most soul-satisfying place on earth? It is reasonable to believe Christ will be found in a place secluded from the noise and confusion of the outside world.

If you still can't believe Christ is actually present in the church, go to a Catholic church, kneel down in a pew, raise up your head toward the altar and say: "Dear Jesus, if you are really present here and want to help me, just let me know somehow, one way or another, that you are really and truly present and will help me. If you don't care to relieve me of my present trial, please give me courage and strength to bear my burden. I will trust in you and will accept whatever you want to do for me."

If you really are sincere in your asking for help and fully believe Christ is present and truly will help you, at this time you will feel and understand the tremendous help Christ has been giving to those who have asked Him for it during the last 2000 years.

WHAT ABOUT JUVENILE DELINQUENTS?

There is so much talk and so many articles written in the papers and magazines about our teen-agers of today, it makes a person wonder about the whole problem.

What is the reason for so much wrongdoing and viciousness by the group of teen-agers who are engaged in these activities?

It doesn't really do much good to make a study of all the things they do. If we add up all the acts of violence and poor behavior, all we get is a picture that gives us a feeling of unpleasantness and sickening despair about the present generation of teen-agers.

It doesn't make any difference how many teen-agers are started on the wrong road through life; there are still a great number who are getting a fairly good start for the proper way of living.

So it seems we have to be thankful that there are so many young people who are doing all right. While we recognize the satisfaction of having a great number of fine young people growing into adults, we still have to face the problem of dealing with those already in trouble.

Let us just develop our thinking along the idea of reporting stories about how tragic the situation of delinquency has become.

We can approach the problem from the negative side, discussing all the evil and tragic results; or we can study the problem from the positive side.

From my reasoning, I find the negative approach cannot or will not accomplish the desired goal in any undertaking. The fact that any situation is terrible or very undesirable does not change anything.

Positive thinking is the only way to change the situation into a new and more desirable one. What can we do to help? That is the real problem we face if we want to do anything for this group of mistaken teen-agers who are making life so hard for themselves.

In the first place, let us decide we shall face the truth. How do our so-called "delinquent teen-agers" behave themselves? Are they doing things that are exactly the same things being done by grown-ups? I am certain the truth is that these teen-agers are following the example set by adults themselves. How can we say it is wrong or terrible for teen-agers to drink and get drunk when there are so many adults who get drunk themselves. What about stealing, fighting, murder, rape, and so forth?

I don't believe we can honestly condemn the teen-agers more than we condemn our adult citizens. In fact, we shouldn't expect as much from youths growing up as we should from adults. The judgment of adults should be better than that of teen-agers.

So it isn't hard to reason out in our minds that we might just as well know that delinquent teen-agers and delinquent adults all fall in the same group. They are all following mistaken ideas and mistaken principles in their living.

A second point of importance is that in spite of all the things teen-agers do that they have no right to do, they still are human beings just like anyone else. They should be respected as creatures of God. What they need is help, not a club over the head. They are already in trouble because they have followed the example set by other human beings.

Let's just try to put ourselves in their position. If we were in such trouble, would it make an impression on us if someone were to do some little kind act to show a little respect for us? If we were knocked down, as they are, would we want someone to give us another kick or would we want them to give us a kind, helping hand? Of course, we would want to be treated with kindness and respect. A respectful act is the right kind of example; it is approaching the problem with a positive attitude.

A third point of importance is that every person is responsible for his own actions exclusively. No person is responsible for the actions of other people. This means we are all responsible for our own actions and accountable only to God. If we do not like the way someone treats us, it always helps to feel we are not responsible for his actions. It is his obligation if he harms us or hurts our feelings. Our duty to ourselves is to stay away from other people who don't like us.

By experience, teen-agers learn they cannot always have their own way about things. With this individual responsibility comes the duty of studying themselves individually, with the purpose of self-improvement.

It is much easier to try to improve ourselves than it is to change the ways of another person.

If I were a teen-ager I would ask myself: Do I have to do what other people do? If the bunch I go with jump in the river, do I have to do the same? Do I have to follow like a lamb? Since I have a free will of my own, I don't have to do something just because other people do it.

Positive thinking could begin at this point. Teen-agers could make up their minds to decide whether an act is worthwhile or not. Certainly anything they do that harms them is not to be considered good for them.

I believe every teen-ager, deep down in his heart and mind, wants two basic freedoms. He wants to be free to think as he pleases. And he wants to act as he pleases.

It is easily understood that many teen-agers are convinced that their parents and other people are trying very hard to keep them from doing what they want to do.

This may be true in many cases. Some parents do want to dominate their children. Of course, normal children do not want to be dominated. So this conflict of minds between the parents and their children can cause a lot of friction in the home.

This friction results in the teen-agers' and their parents' getting further apart, which builds up a loss of confidence in each other.

CAN PARENTS IMPROVE
THEIR POSITION WITH CHILDREN?

1. Parents must realize that there are no fathers or mothers who are perfect.
2. They must also understand that there are no perfect children.
3. Parents do not *own* children.
4. Parents do have custody of children.
5. Parents can teach children honesty only by being honest themselves.

WHAT WILL BE THE COURSE OF
THE CATHOLIC CHURCH IN THE FUTURE?

This is a question that must be in the minds of the leaders of the Church today.

In order to find the answer, the Popes and Church leaders must first find the basic problems that have caused the trouble within the Church.

Why have priests and nuns left the Church? Why were they so dissatisfied that they left after many years of service?

Our reasoning tells us first that many of these priests and nuns probably were never happy with their vocation. A religious life is very different from the way ordinary people live. Those religious leaders who left the Church probably felt that if they got out of their confined way of life, they would be happy.

What they don't realize is this: They may be getting out of the frying pan into the fire. By this I mean the outside world is harder for them to live in than the life inside the Church.

For example, the general public has always looked up to religious leaders and has had quite a bit of respect for them. Now that these priests and nuns have deserted the Church, they will find that they will be treated as ordinary people. Thus, they will miss this respect shown to them so many times before.

Most of them will find life much harder. They will have to start all over in a new way of life. They will not have the feeling of security they have had before.

What can the Catholic church leaders do to prevent this desertion by the priests and nuns? My opinion would be that the Church can't do much about stopping these people from leaving. Right or wrong, they have made up their minds to get out. And so, out they go.

Now we come to the most difficult situation to analyze. Why would these people, who believed they were called by God Himself to become priests and nuns, become so dissatisfied that they would leave their life's work to join the people they were working so hard to help.

Why should marriage be more important to them? Why should freedom to do what they wanted to do be so important? What are they rebelling against?

The most important question seems to be, "Why would anything be more important than serving God Himself?

The Catholic Church has had its ups and downs throughout the last 2,000 years—since Christ was on earth.

I won't say it has had bad Popes or good Popes. The right words would be that some Popes thought and lived as human beings. Other Popes tried to live according to the way God wanted them to think and live.

Through all these years the Catholic Church has been, in my estimation, the finest organization on earth.

The leaders have not always been right in what they believed or what they did. But sincerity has been a very dominating factor in their religious leadership.

The time has now come when the average person in most countries in the world is doing more thinking for himself. He is learning to decide how he thinks about God and religion and many other things. He does not accept the old teachings without question as he used to.

As an individual he feels free to do what he wants to. People have never had this feeling before. There have always been many restraints that people would accept without question.

So now the Catholic Church faces the problems connected with this new questioning and rebellion—this freedom to question what is right or wrong, and then to do what one wants to.

The conflict between scientific discoveries and religious teachings has been going on for many years. Catholic church leaders now face problems of human behavior as well as the scientific discoveries of the present time and the past.

The question of satisfying human beings who are constantly seeking new freedoms and questioning the validity of basic Catholic doctrine becomes more acute as time goes on.

For the church to continue following the same course it has always followed, is not the answer to its problems.

First, the Pope and the rest of the leaders of the Church should teach the fact that God is an unseen, supernatural being. He is the creator of the universe and of everything in the universe. This is an undisputable fact that no thinking human being can deny. All the scientific discoveries that can ever be made will just prove, all the more, the tremendous supernatural creative power that God possesses.

Now, in contrast, let us look at human beings. First, I believe they are the highest form of God's creatures. Just think of all the things they can do. Think of the billions of people God has already created. No two people are ever exactly alike. However, the most important fact to face is that there is no comparison between God and man. Man is the result of the creative power of God.

So, the second important teaching should be that God has complete control over everything He creates. Therefore, God controls every human being on earth. This means that every person on earth must submit to the power of God whether he wants to or not.

Now the third most important fact to teach is that God does not tell human beings: "You do as I tell you or you will be severely punished." God's laws are automatic and must be followed exactly or the human being is automatically starting his own troubles. These laws of God are called the laws of nature. They are found in our minds and our bodies. Also, they are found in all other creations of God. Things we see every day.

All of God's creatures on earth live as God has planned they should, through nature's way on earth.

There is only one exception. Human beings are the only creatures on earth who seek their own way of living. This is because God gave them minds to think and act, each one for himself. Each person is responsible for his own life. No one is responsible for any other person's life.

I believe the Catholic Church will continue as it has for the last 2,000 years. The leaders may be mistaken in some of their ideas, but the Church will continue to exist. The only reason why I make this statement is because the Catholic Church contains Christ Himself in the Holy Eucharist. They recognize the presence of Christ as a supernatural being.

It doesn't make any difference how Christ is there. We don't see Him. We don't hear Him. However, Christ is there in the Church to help any human being who really believes in Him and trusts in Him.

So those people who leave the Church are leaving Christ Himself. They just don't realize how wonderful life is when we trust God and Christ. That is, when we follow His plan for human beings.

The religious leaders are wrong part of the time. God and Christ never make a mistake.

It is all important for Catholic Church leaders to bring their followers to Christ in the Blessed Sacrament. It is up to Christ and God to give human beings the supernatural help that is so necessary for a satisfactory life on earth. Of course this means a sincere submission of their will to Christ and God's will.